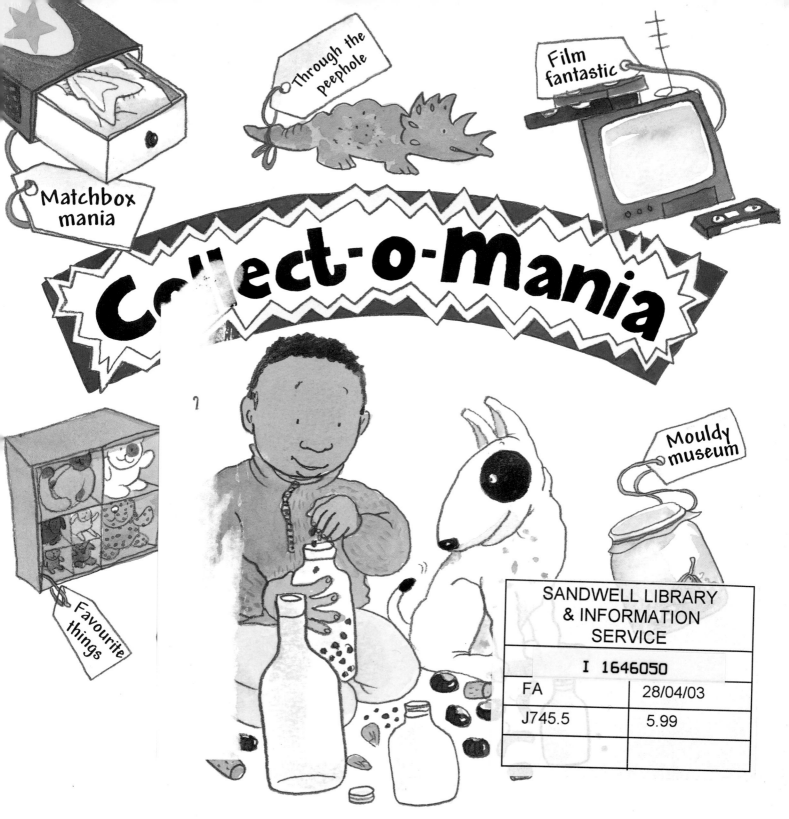

Matchbox mania

Through the peephole

Film fantastic

Favourite things

Mouldy museum

Collect-o-mania

Mick Manning and Brita Granström

W

FRANKLIN WATTS
NEW YORK • LONDON • SYDNEY

Contents

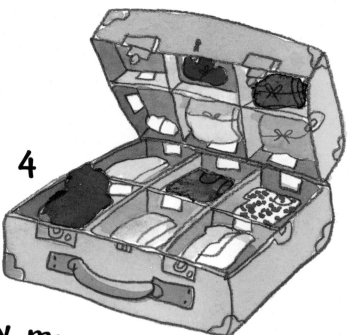

Fingerprint collection

Mouldy museum

Dangling museum

Collect yourself

Be a collect-o-maniac!

Collecting is great fun! You can collect just about anything - from badges and key rings to video clips and mould.
But the best part of being a collect-o-maniac is showing off your collection - you need to make your own museum.
Your museum can be serious, funny, artistic, or even crazy. So long as it displays things to look at, learn about and enjoy, it's a museum!

Museums can be anywhere. You can create large museums in a bedroom, classroom, shed or cellar, or small museums in a matchbox, tin or plastic bottle.

You can even have portable museums and carry around your collection in a suitcase, rucksack or wheelbarrow!

Do you have a favourite hobby or pastime? You could make a collection about it and a museum. Use pictures, words, art and music to help you.

Make sure you know what's in your collection. Write down information on labels about your finds or keep a record in a notebook. When people visit your museum, they can read the labels – or explore your collection just by looking and touching.

Please Touch ↓

welcome to our museum!

You could act out a play with your collection or do a demonstration explaining where you found all your objects and what makes them special. Design a poster for your museum display and hang it up for everyone to see!

5

Portable museum

Portable means something you can carry around. An old suitcase would be very portable - but what sort of museum could you put in it?

1 Divide up your suitcase into compartments. Cut strips of cardboard to fit inside, then slot them together like this.

2 Now add your collection. Cut out pieces of card for labels.

How about a collection of old fashioned clothes - Mum's seventies' tank top or Dad's "punk" T-shirt; or maybe your old baby clothes! You can build on your collection by visiting jumble sales and charity shops.

How about a portable badge collection?

Perhaps you already have some badges that can start your collection. Fasten your badges to the inside lining of a big coat. Then just open your arms wide and hey presto, your museum is open to visitors. This would work well with a button collection too. **Try it out!**

6

Hanging display

Hanging things up is a good way to display a collection. Visitors can get a good look without having to pick anything up. Just hang the objects with string or cotton and dangle a card label a few centimetres below.

Paint the inside of a box. Make holes in the top with a pencil, then thread string through and knot. Attach your finds to the other end.

You could hang a collection of leaves outdoors from a washing line or a low branch to dangle in the breeze.

You could hang plane or bird models from a curtain pole for a window display.

Or why not create a doughnut or bagel display?

If you are going to hang your collection high get help. Don't hang up heavy things.

Mouldy museum

Mould is a sort of tiny fungus that grows on things as they go bad. This is interesting to watch.

An apple will shrink, grow fluffy and turn bright colours as it slowly decays.

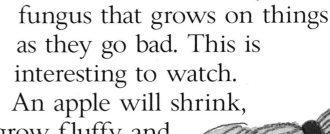

1 Put half of an orange in one jar, an apple piece in another, and a bit of bread or cheese in another.

2 Put kitchen wrap on the jars to keep the strong smells in, but make a tiny airhole in the top. Place the jars on a window sill. Label them and write the date so everyone who visits your museum knows how old the exhibits are.

Always wash your hands after handling decayed food. Keep your museum away from any fresh food. Food decay can causes food poisoning, and that can make you very ill.

For a permanent collection, try drawing or photographing the changes that happen.

11

Through the peephole

Make an imaginary world with your collection. Use your toy dinosaurs to take you time travelling back to the Jurassic age! Try making an underwater world, a haunted castle or even a "lost in space" scene.

1 Find a box with a lid. Cut out holes around the side to peep through (you'll need help). Cut two large holes in the lid to let in light but tape tracing or greaseproof paper over them so that people can't peek.

2 For a Jurassic world, make a scene with pebbles, twigs and leaves. Use Plasticine to position them in the box. Hide your dinosaurs in the scene. Tape on the lid.

3 Hold the box under a light or near a window and your visitors can peep through into a Jurassic world: it's exciting and a bit scary! Play some music to make it more atmospheric. What music do you think would go well with dinosaurs?

13

Short life collection

This means a collection that will only last a few weeks, days, hours or even a few minutes - that's the fun of it! A short life museum could be almost anywhere: in your garden, backyard, window sill, or even on a beach.

Seaside collection

Make a collection of beach finds and place them along the seashore. Use a stick to write labels and perhaps some facts about them in the sand. Now you have a seaside museum for passers-by to look at until the tide comes in and washes it away!

Don't touch anything sharp or any needles you may find.

Backyard museum

Make a sculpture or display from kitchen scraps and peanuts. How long before it disappears thanks to birds and other wildlife?

Make a list of who visits your museum, and who eats what. Clear away any food at the end of the day so you don't attract rats!

Ice age

Keep a collection on ice! Ice stops things decaying. Sometimes animals and even people from long ago are found buried in the ancient ice of cold countries. Your visitors can make their own ice age discoveries!

On a snowy day, make some snow heads and use them to model a collection of hats or spectacles.

Make an ice bowl

❶ Take some tiny plastic animals, shells and tiny pebbles and place them in an ice cube tray with water. Put the tray in the freezer.

❷ When the ice has set, take out the cubes and arrange them in a bowl. Slowly the objects will melt free from their icy prison just like real ice age remains do.

Make an ice bowl to hold your museum. You need two freezer-proof bowls, one a bit smaller than the other. Pour water in the bigger bowl and press the smaller bowl into it, holding it down with masking tape. You can drop berries or petals into the water. Freeze overnight.

Fingerprint collection

Everybody has a different pattern on their fingers - that's why the police use fingerprints to identify criminals. Fingerprints are like signatures. Why not collect them instead of autographs? They are just as unique and more fun!

grandad

my aunt

grar

mum dad

my baby sister

me

my brother

You could make a family tree museum with fingerprints.

You can buy an ink pad from a stationery shop or make prints by pressing your fingertips in paint and then printing. Do some test prints first.

You could make a fingerprint book. Write each person's name next to their prints.

Make a chart of the prints of your classmates – collect hand- and footprints too.

19

Touch and feel

We all use touch to help us find out about objects. See if your visitors can name the objects in your touch collection. You'll find some ordinary things can feel quite scary and strange!

Find some boxes and cut a hole in the front just big enough to squeeze a hand inside!

In each box put an object with a different texture like:

something fluffy and soft, such as a cuddly toy;

something natural – a handful of dead leaves and twigs or a feather;

something prickly, like a hairbrush.

Try something scary or slimy like a toy spider or even jelly!

21

Smell exhibition

Smell is one of our senses, although a dog's sense of smell is a million times better than our own! Make a smell exhibition for your family and friends and check out their sense of smell. Ask an adult to help you choose your smell selection to make sure it is safe.

Make a collection of strong smells like perfume, aftershave, spices, herbs, cheese, garlic and coffee. You can also have some delicate smells like rose petals or tea.

Put each "smell" in a different bottle and wrap the bottle with paper so your museum visitors cannot see what's inside. Write a number on each bottle. Keep a list of numbers and smells and then invite your visitors to sniff and guess what's inside. Keep a score of right and wrong answers!

23

Sound gallery

Make a sound gallery to entertain yourself and your visitors. Start collecting old spoons, cardboard tubes, nuts and bolts and you can make an orchestra.

Stretch some greaseproof paper or a bin bag tightly over an empty biscuit tin and tape the sides. Now bang it with a wooden spoon and you have a drum!

You can make dangling chimes like this using a coat hanger. Hang jingly objects on it like small bells. Hang them outdoors in the breeze, or indoors where you can hear them chime!

Make some shakers

Fill two empty plastic bottles with some dried peas or small stones. Fix the lid on and you have a pair of maracas. Now you can invite your visitors to join in and make some noise!

Roll a piece of card into a cone. Paint it a bright colour or decorate it with silver foil and you have a megaphone!

Film fantastic

Who is your favourite film star, TV personality or cartoon character? Do you cut out clippings about the team you support, or watch all the programmes about your favourite wild animal? Why not make this the beginning of your own film museum.

film museum

Make a video scrapbook by recording clips. You could have a video of great goals, a collection of tiger documentaries or interviews with a pop star.

Have a film show. Make an invitation saying what's on, when and where and give them to your friends. You could also make a film club poster like this.

Ticket
Ticket
Ticket
Ticket
Ticket

Keep a scrapbook of the programmes you watch. Remember to put in the ones you don't like as well – so you can compare good and bad.

first rattle

my first shoe

my dummy

...of hair

my favourite car

1 school badge

my troll + pencil from ...ool

my teeth

love football

Collect yourself

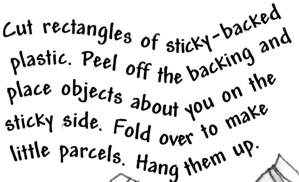

Make a collection about yourself. Start right away by finding some photos of yourself from when you were a baby. Keep them in a photo album or scrapbook.

Cut rectangles of sticky-backed plastic. Peel off the backing and place objects about you on the sticky side. Fold over to make little parcels. Hang them up.

Small freezer bags with snap fasteners are good to keep things in.

Store old letters, postcards and school reports in a box file or tin. Don't just keep the good things — include injection certificates, even scabs or fallen-out teeth!

Make a scrapbook with souvenirs about your life.

Pickle it!

A pickled museum would make a nice present for someone and looks good displayed on a window sill. These pickles aren't for eating, though. Remember some wild plants and nuts are poisonous.

1 Collect and wash some bottles or jam jars. Half fill them with pickling vinegar; use a funnel to make it easier.

3 Top up the bottles with vinegar if you need to, then screw the caps on tight. Add sticky labels.

2 Now drop in your collection. It can be acorns, conkers, flower petals or leaves. You can even pickle small dead insects like ladybirds, but only if you find them dead. Never pick wild flowers or kill anything!

Vinegar is very strong. Wash your hands after using it and don't get it near your eyes.

31

Packaging collection

Boxes, cartons, packets and sweet wrappers are interesting to collect. Designs change so quickly that in a short time your boxes will become old-fashioned — and you'll have a collection of antiques!

Store your packs in a "fridge". Make one from a large box. Ask someone to cut a door and wedge cardboard strips inside for shelves.

Open both ends of any boxes and flatten them for easy storage. Make sure any bottles or containers are clean and dry.

Candy moulds

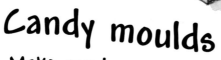

Make candy shapes to fill empty chocolate box trays. Mix some plaster of paris (buy this from a chemist) with some water until you have a creamy mixture.

Spoon the mixture into the holes in the trays. When the plaster is dry (it doesn't take long) you can push them out of the moulds. Now decorate them!

33

Nature table

Have you been to a nature museum and seen dusty glass cases full of stuffed animals? Nature collections don't have to be like that - yours can much more exciting! You can display all sorts of nature finds such as feathers, pebbles, fossils, bird skulls and bones.

Put a small piece of meat on a pot of soil outdoors. Ask an adult to cut a plastic bottle in half. Place it over the meat. Flies will enter the bottle and lay eggs in the meat.

In a few days you can see maggots hatching.

Arrange all your objects on a paper tablecloth and write labels. Now draw around each shape so if you have to put your finds away you can put them back in the right place again.

Press leaves between kitchen paper in a book. Stick them onto card and label them. Explain where you found them.

Dangling museum

Earrings and key-rings are fun to collect - and if you go fishing, what about a safe way to show off your lures, flies and floats?

Hang key-rings from small pins stuck in a cork pinboard.

Fishing lures and flies can be beautiful objects, but watch out – they have sharp hooks! You can show them off and keep your fingers safe.

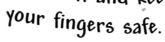

Find a piece of polystyrene. Push the hooks into the material. Hang this display board out of reach of any younger brothers or sisters.

Pin sheets of card to your wall so that the edges overlap. Along the bottom of each sheet make a row of holes to hang earrings from.

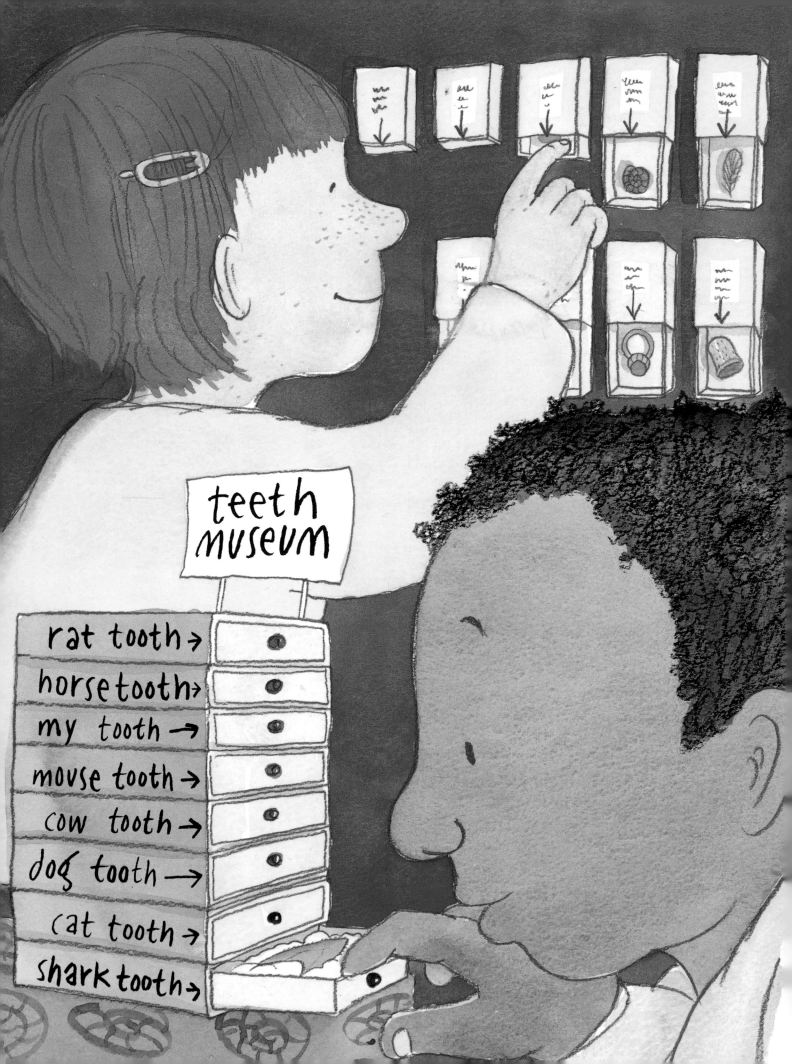

Matchbox mania

Empty matchboxes are good fun to collect. You can fill them with tiny things such as shells, small beads or feathers.

You can stick your matchboxes onto a piece of card or onto a wall (ask first!). Draw arrows to show your visitors which way they open and close.

Display case

1 Collect a number of empty matchboxes and take out their drawers. Now glue them together – one on top of the other. PVA glue is best for this job.

2 Ask someone to poke a hole in the front of drawers, then push in a paper fastener to make a tiny handle.

3 Slide the drawers back to finish off your display case. You can decorate it too.

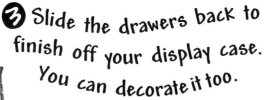

Never play with matches; you might start a fire.

Favourite things

Do you have a collection of favourite things? Maybe it's teddies, toy elephants or miniature pottery animals. Why not make a display cabinet for them?

❶ Find a large cardboard box and some smaller boxes to go inside. Now fit the smaller boxes into the large one.

It's a bit like a jigsaw puzzle.

Boxes that have held glasses or crockery are good for displays as they are divided already.

Glue empty matchbox trays into the lid of a shoe box to make a display case for tiny things.

❷ Once you are satisfied with the arrangement of the boxes dab on some PVA glue to stick them together.

41

Dig it up!

This is a bit like being an archaeologist. An archaeologist is someone who digs up things from long ago, like dinosaur bones or old coins.

Do a treasure hunt – bury some stones and one "precious" bead. Who will find the treasure first?

Find some deep trays or strong cardboard boxes and half fill them with sand or soil.

Now bury some interesting objects like toy dinosaurs, plastic jewellery or shells. Cover them up with more soil or sand.

Invite your friends to join you in a "dig". You are only allowed to use teaspoons!

Museum in a book

You could call a diary a sort of museum: it's a collection of your day-to-day thoughts and activities! Store your videotape, cassette or written diary inside an old book, then it really is a museum in a book!

What about making a tape recorder diary. Tell it your thoughts about the things that happen in your life.

Or you could make a video diary of an event like Christmas or a visit to the seaside.

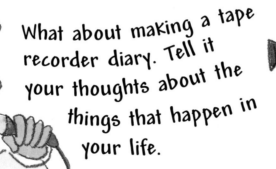

Museum in a book

Find a fat old book from a jumble sale or charity shop, check no one else wants it and stick all the pages together with glue.

When the glue is dry, ask an adult to help you cut a square hole inside the book – just big enough for your diary to fit secretly inside.

Make a catalogue

Collections and museums often have a catalogue. A catalogue is a book or pamphlet that lists everything in the collection - telling visitors what the exhibits are and where they are from. Catalogues can be simple lists or beautifully illustrated books.

1 You can make your own catalogue of exhibits. Use a large piece of paper to list all your objects; you can then add pictures, photos and even stories about how you found them.

2 Fold the paper over to make a little booklet

3 Use a stapler to keep the pages together or you can even sew down one edge with colourful thread.

4 Make your catalogue cover eye-catching. Glue on sand or glitter, or try sticking on fur fabric or shells.

Index

To Paula Borton - MM & BG

This edition 2003
Franklin Watts, 96 Leonard Street, London EC2A 4XD
Franklin Watts Australia, 45-51 Huntley Street,
Alexandria, NSW 2015
Text and illustrations Copyright © Mick Manning and
Brita Granström 1998, 2003

Editor: Paula Borton; Art director: Robert Walster
First published under the title *Collect-o-Mania*
A CIP record is available from the British Library.
Dewey Classification 069
Printed in Dubai
ISBN 0 7496 5048 6